BALLET

LET'S DANCE

Tracy M. Maurer

The Rourke Press, Inc.
Vero Beach, Florida 32964

© 1997 The Rourke Press, Inc.

Tracy M. Maurer, author of the Dance Series, specializes in non-fiction and business writing. She has previously worked with several educational organizations on various writing projects, including creating classroom workbooks for elementary students. Tracy's most recently published hard cover book focused on the city of Macon, Georgia. A graduate of the University of Minnesota - Minneapolis School of Journalism, she now lives in Park Falls, Wisconsin, with her husband Mike.

PHOTO CREDITS
All photos © Timothy L. Vacula except © Lois M. Nelson: page 17

EDITORIAL SERVICES:
Penworthy Learning Systems and Lois M. Nelson

With appreciation to Jane Madison, The Madison Studio, Macon, GA; Sharona Paller Rubinstein, The Macon Moving Company, Macon, GA

Library of Congress Cataloging-in-Publication Data

Maurer, Tracy, 1965-
    Ballet / Tracy M. Maurer.
        p. cm. — (Let's dance)
    Includes index
    Summary: Discusses ballet training and techniques, shoes, music and other related topics.
    ISBN 1-57103-170-7
    1. Ballet—Juvenile literature. 2. Ballet dancing—Juvenile literature. [1. Ballet dancing] I. Title II. Series: Maurer, Tracy, 1965- Let's dance.
GV1787.5.M38 1997
792.8—dc21   97-8396
                                                   CIP
                                                   AC

Printed in the USA

TABLE OF CONTENTS

BALLET IS SPECIAL

Ballet is a special kind of dance that blends movement with music, art, and drama. Dancers perform the steps in much the same way all over the world.

Ballet dancers turn their legs out at the hips so that their feet point away from each other in a line. This "turn out" makes ballet different from other dances. Another difference is the **pointe** (POYNT), or dance steps on the tips of the shoes.

Both boy and girl ballet dancers "turn-out" their hips, but boys almost never dance en pointe.

HOW BALLET BEGAN

Ballet began in the courts of Italy and France more than 400 years ago. At first only men and boys danced in ballets. They were often kings and princes. King Louis XIV of France, a famous dancer in the 1600s, started a ballet school that made France the first center of ballet.

French became ballet's language. Today dancers must learn many French words, such as **plié** (plee AY), meaning knee bend. They also learn the *same* ballet rules made by King Louis' dance instructor!

Ballet dancers learn the same foot and hand positions everywhere in the world.

LESSONS FROM EXPERIENCE

Young ballet students have always needed experienced ballet dancers for lessons. Reading a full ballet written on paper takes special training.

Students watch their teachers to see how to perform the ballet movements.

Special exercises help young dancers build strength and move with grace. Students also gain **stamina** (STAM uh nuh) to keep dancing without getting tired. Most dancers practice every day.

A ballet student practices a dance position with her teacher.

PRACTICING AT THE BARRE

Dancers go to classes held in a studio. Large mirrors in the studio let students see to correct themselves.

Dancers hold the **barre** (BAHR), a wooden bar on the walls, for balance during warm-up exercises.

Students learn new movements and practice jumps at the center of the studio. They start with small jumps and work up to higher ones. Classes end with a **révérence** (reh VER ahns), a bow or curtsey to thank the teacher.

Physical training for all ballet dancers includes warm-up exercises at the barre.

Modern ballet dancers often use steps from other kinds of dances. They rarely wear tutus or other traditional costumes.

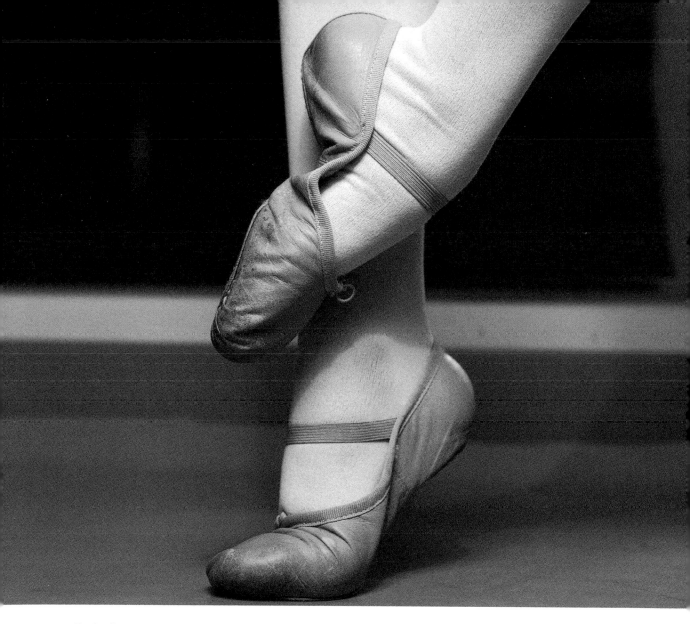

Soft, flat ballet shoes let the dancer's feet flex, or bend, to help build muscles in the feet and ankles.

THE FIRST STEPS

Just as you learn letters before spelling words, dancers must master five foot positions before learning ballet steps. The legs turn out from the hips in all the positions. The feet move closer or further apart to form each position.

Nearly every ballet step begins and ends in one of the five positions. When dancers jump, they sometimes move to one of the positions in the air. Ballerinas also learn to perform all five positions en pointe or **relevé** (reh luh VAY).

After a ballerina masters the five foot positions in her flat ballet shoes, she learns to perform all of them en pointe.

WATCH THE HANDS

Ballet has five arm positions. Dancers gently curve their fingers and relax their thumbs in every arm position.

In time, boys learn big, bolder arm movements. Ballerinas do not. They learn to perform delicate **gestures** (JES churz).

Some ballets tell a story with **mime** (MYM), or hand and arm actions that have meanings. For example, pointing to yourself means "me" or "I" in mime.

Slightly curved fingers give ballet dancers a graceful look, even when the ballet movements are difficult.

FLAT AND POINTE SHOES

All new ballet dancers wear flat ballet shoes. At about ten years of age and after many years of training, girls learn to dance on their toes with pointe shoes. Dancing in pointe shoes too soon can hurt the feet, hips, or back.

A block of glued satin, paper, and rough fabric fills the toe of each pointe shoe. New shoes have no left or right. Instead, they form to the ballerina's feet. A ballerina may keep ten or more pointe shoes ready to wear for performances.

New pointe shoes feel stiff until they form to the ballerina's foot.

BALLET MUSIC

A **choreographer** (KAWR ee OG ruh fur) creates the dances and action for each ballet. He or she can choose any type of music to use with the ballet, such as classical music played by an orchestra or new music written just for that ballet.

The ballet dancing and the music flow together. A man dancing a solo may jump higher as the music grows louder. A couple dancing together in the last scene, called a **finale** (fuh NAL ee), might match grand lifts to the ending music.

Exercises help prepare young boys and girls for the ballet dances they may perform together when they grow up.

WHERE TO SEE BALLET

Ballet is exciting to watch. Costumes sometimes give clues about the ballet. Ballerinas wear long **tutus**(TOO tooz), or dresses with layers of net, most often in romantic ballets. They usually wear short, stiff tutus in classical ballets. You might see **unitards** (YOO ni TAHRDZ), or one-piece body suits, in modern ballets.

Theaters around the world host ballets. TV programs and videos also show them. Visit the library to learn about each ballet's story before you see it and to find more books about the beauty of ballet.

Glossary

barre (BAHR) — a wooden bar on the walls of a dance studio that students use for balance

choreographer (KAWR ee OG ruh fur) — the person who selects music and creates dance steps and actions for a ballet

finale (fuh NAL ee) — the last part of a ballet

gestures (JES chur) — hand or arm movements

mime (MYM) — hand or arm movements that have meanings; ballet mimes often act out their parts of a story without dancing

plié (plee AY) — a knee bend with a straight back

pointe (POYNT) — the tips of the toes; ballerinas dance en pointe, on their toes, in special pointe shoes

relevé (reh luh VAY) — raised up on the toes

révérence (reh VER ahns) — a bow or curtsey to thank the teacher at the end of a ballet class

stamina (STAM uh nuh) — the energy to keep moving without getting tired

tutus (TOO tooz) — dress-like costumes with layers of net in the skirt

unitards (YOO ni TAHRDZ) — one-piece costumes that fit tightly

INDEX